AMERICAN HEROES

BOOKER T. WASHINGTON

Getting into the Schoolhouse

AMERICAN HEROES

BOOKER T. WASHINGTON

Getting into the Schoolhouse

LARRY DANE BRIMNER

Marshall Cavendish
Benchmark

New York

For Sneed B. Collard III,
environmental steward and valued friend

Marshall Cavendish Benchmark
99 White Plains Road
Tarrytown, New York 10591
www.marshallcavendish.us

Library of Congress Cataloging-in-Publication Data
Brimner, Larry Dane.
Booker T. Washington : getting into the schoolhouse / by Larry Dane Brimner.
p. cm. — (American heroes)
Summary: "A juvenile biography of Booker T. Washington, who rose from slavery to become a great African-American leader and educator"—Provided by publisher. Includes bibliographical references and index.
ISBN 978-0-7614-3063-6
1. Washington, Booker T., 1856-1915—Juvenile literature. 2. African Americans—Biography—Juvenile literature.
3. Educators—United States—Biography—Juvenile literature. I. Title.
E185.97.W4B75 2009
370.92—dc22
[B]
2008002870

Editor: Joyce Stanton
Publisher: Michelle Bisson
Art Director: Anahid Hamparian
Designer: Anne Scatto
Printed in Malaysia
135642

TITLE PAGE: *Booker T. Washington Legend,* by William H. Johnson, African-American artist
BACK COVER: A hand-painted photo of Armstrong Hall, built by students at the Tuskegee Institute

Images provided by Debbie Needleman, Picture Researcher, Portsmouth, NH, from the following sources:
Front Cover: The Granger Collection, New York. *Back Cover:* North Wind Picture Archives. *Pages i, 13, 36:* The Granger Collection, New York; *page ii:* Smithsonian American Art Museum, Washington, D.C./Art Resource, NY; *page vi:* Library of Congress Prints and Photographs Division, Washington, D.C.; *page 1:* Ohio Historical Society; *page 3:* The White House; *pages 4, 16, 23:* North Wind Picture Archives; *pages 7, 8, 20, 31:* Booker T. Washington and Frank Beard, 1901. *An Autobiography: The Story of My Life and Work.* Documenting the American South. University Library. The University of North Carolina at Chapel Hill; *page 11:* 2008 Michael Escoffery/Artists Rights Society (ARS), New York/Art Resource/NY; *pages 15, 33:* CORBIS; *page 19:* Virginia Historical Society, Richmond, Virginia; *page 23 inset:* Courtesy of Hampton University Archives; *pages 24, 27, 28:* Booker T. Washington. 1901. *Up From Slavery:* An Autobiography. Documenting the American South. University Library. The University of North Carolina at Chapel Hill; *page 35:* Thomas S. England/Time Life Pictures/Getty Images

CONTENTS

Through knowledge, Booker believed, African Americans would gain equality.

Booker T. Washington

A leader. A teacher. A popular public speaker. Booker T. Washington was all of these things.

Booker T. Washington had a deep hunger for learning. He valued hard work and took pride in doing a job correctly. Most of all, he believed that through knowledge and skills, African Americans would gain equality.

Booker was born a slave, most likely in 1856. No one is certain of the exact date. A slave's birth wasn't important enough to record.

He was born in a small log cabin on a Virginia plantation near Hale's Ford. Later, Booker recalled that gaps between the logs "let in the light, and also the cold, chilly air of winter." At night, he slept with his older brother John and his sister Amanda "upon a bundle of filthy rags" piled on the dirt floor.

Booker was born in this log cabin around the year 1856.

The son of a slave, Booker was a slave, too. His days were filled with chores.

Booker's childhood was filled with chores. He cleaned the yard around his master's house. He carried water to slaves working in the fields. Of all his chores, the one he disliked most was taking corn to the mill. The heavy bag of corn was thrown across the back of a horse. Almost without fail, it would slip to the ground along the way. Booker was too small to place it back upon the horse. He would have to wait for someone to help him. This made him late getting home, and his master would scold or whip him because of it.

People were starting to change the way they thought about slavery. In the North, most people wanted slavery to end. In the South, it was a different story. Slaves were vital to the South's economy and way of life. It was slaves who planted the cotton and tobacco fields, and harvested them. The South voted to break away from the United States and, in 1861, the War Between the States—the Civil War—began.

Booker's mother, Jane, prayed that the North—the Union—would win. Then she and her children would be free.

Booker's mother prayed that the North would win the Civil War.

As a boy, Booker wanted more than anything to learn how to read.

With a war on, Booker now had to walk his master's daughter to school to make sure she got there safely. It was against the law for slaves to go to school, so Booker couldn't stay. But sometimes he would peek through the window and see the children reading their books. He thought "to get into a schoolhouse and study in this way would be about the same as getting into paradise."

In April 1865, the Civil War ended when General Robert E. Lee surrendered to Ulysses S. Grant, the Union general. The North had won. This meant that the United States would be whole again.

It also meant that, at last, all the slaves were free!

When the slaves were set free, they danced for joy.

That summer Booker's family left Virginia to join his stepfather in Malden, West Virginia. In Malden, Booker had to help support his family—and he also finally got his chance to go to school. He worked in a salt mine from four o'clock until nine o'clock in the morning. He went to school the rest of the day.

Like this man who had no special skills,
Booker had to work in a salt mine to earn money.

It was at school that Booker noticed that the other children had two names. When the teacher asked him his name, he replied, "Booker Washington."

Washington was his stepfather's first name, and Booker liked the sound of it. Some time later his mother explained to him that his second name was Taliaferro. That's how he became Booker T. Washington.

Finally, Booker got his chance to go to school.

*At the Hampton Institute, African Americans could learn
the skills they needed to get good jobs.*

Soon, though, Booker had to quit school to haul coal. It was dirty work, but he learned something in the coal mine that would change his life forever. He overheard two miners talking about the Hampton Institute, a school in Virginia for African Americans. It was a school that could teach him what he needed to know to get a good job.

Booker thought about the Hampton Institute while he hauled coal. He thought about it later when he went to work for Viola Ruffner, the wife of the man who owned the coal mine.

Mrs. Ruffner had already hired and fired a number of servants when Booker came to work for her. She demanded honesty and that a job be done correctly. These were important lessons that Booker never forgot.

For Booker, the Hampton Institute was a faraway dream.

One day, Booker decided to make his way
to the Hampton Institute.

Booker was now sixteen years old. He decided he should give the Hampton Institute a try. It was five hundred miles away, back in Virginia. It took him a long time to get there. He took a train, he took a stagecoach, and he walked. And walked. Booker walked nearly a hundred miles. When he finally arrived at the Hampton Institute on October 5, 1872, he was tired and dirty. The head teacher, Miss Mary Mackie, had doubts about him. As a test, she told him to sweep the classroom next door.

Booker remembered what Mrs. Ruffner had taught him. He swept and dusted until the room almost shone. When Miss Mackie returned to inspect his work, she rubbed a handkerchief over the woodwork. "I guess you will do to enter this institution," she said.

A photo of Miss Mary Mackie

Miss Mackie tested Booker by having him sweep and dust a classroom.
Only then would she admit him to the school.

After studying at the Hampton Institute,
Booker became a fine teacher.

By the time Booker left the Hampton Institute three years later, he had learned the lessons in books. He had become an able speaker. He had also learned how to use a napkin, a toothbrush, and the sheets on a bed.

What was next?

Booker returned to Malden to teach. "I taught any one who wanted to learn anything that I could teach him," he said later.

Booker's star was about to rise. In the summer of 1879, he returned to the Hampton Institute—this time as a teacher. When some gentlemen in Alabama wanted a person to start a school for African Americans, they wrote to the Hampton Institute for a recommendation. They were told that the only man for the job was Booker T. Washington.

Samuel Chapman Armstrong, founder of the Hampton Institute, recommended Booker as the best man to start a school in Tuskegee, Alabama.

Booker found only a couple of buildings and an old church when he got to Tuskegee.

Booker arrived in Tuskegee, Alabama, in 1881. He expected to find at least a schoolhouse, but he found "nothing of the kind." He went to work raising money and opened the Tuskegee Institute on July 4, 1881, with thirty students in a rundown church.

Booker worked hard and his little school grew. He decided it was time to look for a wife, and he married in 1882. Soon his family started to grow, too. A baby girl the couple named Portia was born the next year. Sadly, his wife died in 1884. A year later he married again—a teacher at the Tuskegee Institute—and before long two sons joined the Washington family. After the death of his second wife, he married a third time, in 1893. During all these years, despite his personal misfortunes, Booker worked tirelessly to lift African Americans out of poverty through education.

Booker's family grew to include a daughter and two sons.
Here he is shown with his third wife, Margaret.

Not everyone agreed with Booker's thoughts on education. Some people said he spent too much time teaching African Americans to work with their hands. Booker didn't feel that way. He believed that the best path to equality was by being skilled in a trade, such as carpentry or cooking. That way, he thought, a person had a better chance of getting work.

Booker believed that the best path to equality was having a skill that could earn a person a good living.

Booker T. Washington died in 1915 at the age of fifty-nine. By then, the little school in Tuskegee had grown from 30 to 1,500 students—and more than one hundred buildings.

Today, Tuskegee University carries on his tradition of progress and equality through knowledge.

Booker continued to lead the Tuskegee Institute until he died. The work he did will never be forgotten.

IMPORTANT DATES

1856 Born a slave in Hale's Ford, Virginia.

1861 The Civil War breaks out in the United States between the North and the South.

1865 The Civil War ends. Booker and his family move to Malden, West Virginia, to join stepfather, Washington Ferguson.

1872 Enters Hampton Institute; works as a janitor to earn his tuition and expenses.

1875 Returns to Malden to teach.

1879 Begins teaching at Hampton Institute.

1881 Opens Tuskegee Institute in Tuskegee, Alabama, to train African-American teachers.

1882 Marries Fannie Smith. Daughter, Portia, is born the next year.

1884 Fannie dies.

1885 Marries Olivia Davidson.

1887 Son Booker T. Washington Jr. is born.

1889 Son Ernest Davidson is born. Olivia dies.

1893 Marries Margaret Murray.

1901 Publishes his autobiography, *Up from Slavery.*

1915 Dies on November 13 at age fifty-nine.

WORDS TO KNOW

Civil War The war in the United States between the North and the South that was fought, in part, over slavery from 1861 to 1865.

economy The way in which a place earns its money.

institute A college for learning skills.

misfortune Something that is hard to bear; bad luck.

plantation A large farm.

recommendation A suggestion.

slave A person who is owned by another person.

Union The United States of America; the states that were opposed to slavery during the Civil War.

To Learn More about Booker T. Washington

WEB SITES

biography.com:
http://www.biography.com/search/article.do?id=9524663

Booker T. Washington Virtual Museum and Storybook:
http://score.rims.k12.ca.us/activity/bookertwashington

Gale CENGAGE Learning:
http://www.galegroup.com/free_resources/bhm/bio/
washington_b.htm

The Progress of a People:
http://lcweb2.loc.gov/ammem/aap/bookert.html

BOOKS

Booker T. Washington: Great American Educator by Eric Braun,
Capstone Press, 2006.

Booker T. Washington: Leader and Educator by Pat and Fredrick
McKissack, Enslow Elementary, revised 2001.

Booker T. Washington: A Photo-Illustrated Biography by Margo
McLoone, Capstone Press, 2000.

A Hunger for Learning: A Story about Booker T. Washington by
Gwenyth Swain and Larry Johnson, Lerner Publications, 2005.

PLACES TO VISIT

Booker T. Washington National Monument
12130 Booker T. Washington Highway
Hardy, VA 24101
PHONE: (540) 721-2094
WEB SITE: http://www.nps.gov/bowa

Tuskegee University
PO Box 1239
Tuskegee, AL 36088
PHONE: (334) 727-8501
WEB SITE: http://www.tuskegee.edu

INDEX

Page numbers for illustrations are in boldface.

A Note on Quotes

Booker T. Washington published his autobiography, *Up from Slavery*, in 1901. The quotations in this book come from the Signet Classic edition published in 2000.

ABOUT THE AUTHOR

LARRY DANE BRIMNER is the author of almost 150 books for children, many of them award-winners. Among his fiction and nonfiction titles are *A Migrant Family*, an NCSS/CBC Notable Trade Book in the Field of Social Studies; *The Littlest Wolf,* an IRA/CBC Children's Choice book, Oppenheim Gold Medal recipient, and 2004 Great Lakes' Great Books (Michigan) Honor book; and *Subway: The Story of Tunnels, Tubes, and Tracks*, a Junior Library Guild selection. Larry makes his home in Tucson, Arizona. To learn more about him, investigate his Web site at www.brimner.com.